# THE LOCK & THE KEY
Sexual Mores in the Last Days

For My Parents

Louis & Evelyn Goldstein

**ISBN-10: 0692237852**
**ISBN-13: 978-0692237854**

**The Lock & The Key**
Sheila R. Vitale

Christ-Centered Kabbalah
**Sheila R. Vitale**
P O Box 562
Port Jefferson Station, NY 11776-0562
(631) 331-1493

# Christ-Centered Kabbalah

**Sheila R. Vitale**
**Pastor, Teacher, Founder**
PO Box 562
Port Jefferson Station, NY 11776 USA

EXCERPT FROM
Session 1 of
MESSAGE #801- Part 6
THE WOMAN & THE BEAST

**Edited and Adapted as a Book by**
**Sheila R. Vitale**

# THE LOCK & THE KEY
## Sexual Mores in the Last Days

The Following Excerpt Has Been Transcribed and
Edited For Clarity, Continuity of Thought, And Punctuation By

**The CCK Transcribing and Editing Team**

# Christ-Centered Kabbalah

~ The Compleat Kabbalah ~

## Sheila R. Vitale
### Pastor, Teacher & Founder

## Ministry Staff
Anthony Milton, Teacher (South Carolina)
Brooke Paige, Teacher (New York)
Sandra Aldrich (MN) (July 7, 1975 – April 18, 2021)

## Administrative Staff
Susan Panebianco, Office Manager

## Editorial Staff
Rose Herczeg, Editor

## Technical Staff
Lape Mobolaji-Lawal, Database Administrator

## Ministry Illustrators
Cecilia H. Bryant (Oct. 18, 1921 – Oct. 23, 2013)
Fidelis Onwubueke

## Music Staff
June Eble, Singer, Lyricist and Clarinetist
(July 20, 1931 – Jan. 24, 2024)
Don Gervais, Singer, Lyricist and Guitarist
Rita L. Rora, Singer, Lyricist and Guitarist

# Table of Contents

# The Alternate Translation Bible©

***The Alternate Translation Bible* (ATB)** is an original
interpretation of the Scripture.
**It is not intended to replace traditional translations**.

Alternate Translation of the Old Testament©
Alternate Translation, Exodus, Chapter 32
    (Crime of the Calf)©
Alternate Translation, Daniel, Chapter 8©
Alternate Translation, Daniel, Chapter 11©
Alternate Translation, Genesis 9:18-27
    (The Noah Chronicles, Second Edition) ©


Alternate Translation of the New Testament©
Alternate Translation, 2 Thessalonians, Chapter 2
    (Sophia)©
Alternate Translation, 1ˢᵗ John, Chapter 5©
Alternate Translation, the Book of Colossians
    (To The Church At Colosse) ©
Alternate Translation, the Book of Ephesians
    (To The Church At Ephesus) ©
Alternate Translation, the Book of Corinthians, Chapter 11
    (Corinthian Confusion) ©
Alternate Translation, the Book of Jude
    (The Common Salvation)©


Alternate Translation of the Book of the Revelation of Jesus Christ
    to St. John©
Traducción Alternada del Libro de Revelación de Jesucristo©

# Alternate Translations in This Book

# THE LOCK & THE KEY
## Sexual Mores in the Last Days

# Emotions & Lust

### 2 Pet 1:4 – *Escape From Lust*

> **4** WHEREBY ARE GIVEN UNTO US EXCEEDING GREAT AND PRECIOUS PROMISES: THAT BY THESE YE MIGHT BE PARTAKERS OF THE DIVINE NATURE, **HAVING ESCAPED THE CORRUPTION THAT IS IN THE WORLD THROUGH LUST.** **KJV**

No matter how good our intentions are, we can be corrupted by the lust which rules this world through our emotions. There are emotions inside of us which lust for things God says we should not have, and they corrupt us. Whether we act on them or not, they violate the Spirit of God within us. They corrupt us. They make us unclean.

The Lord Jesus Christ is joining himself to these ungodly powers in us, the source of our ungodly actions, these ungodly emotions in us, and making them Godly. He is not destroying them. He is taking what is unclean and he is cleaning it. Jesus said to his disciples after he washed their feet, *you are now wholly clean; every whit clean*.

### Jn 13:10 – *Cleansed From Sin*

> **10** JESUS SAITH TO HIM, HE THAT IS WASHED NEEDETH NOT SAVE TO WASH HIS FEET, BUT IS CLEAN EVERY WHIT: AND **YE ARE CLEAN,** BUT NOT ALL. **KJV**

Jesus' disciples were not made clean because Jesus washed their physical feet. That is a parable. Did Jesus wash their physical feet? In my opinion, he probably did not. Jesus revealed sin in his disciples and attached his soul (which was righteous because it was joined to Jehovah) to their emotions, the source of the lust which corrupts us.

There are seven degrees of pride which corrupt us when we fail to control our emotions. We are made every whit whole, every whit clean, when the Lord Jesus Christ joins Christ Jesus, his Son, to the seven emotions of our fallen nature.

### Pro 6:16-19 – *Seven Deadly Sins*

16 THESE SIX THINGS DOTH THE LORD HATE: YEA, SEVEN ARE AN ABOMINATION UNTO HIM:

17 A PROUD LOOK, A LYING TONGUE, AND HANDS THAT SHED INNOCENT BLOOD,

18 AN HEART THAT DEVISETH WICKED IMAGINATIONS, FEET THAT BE SWIFT IN RUNNING TO MISCHIEF,

19 A FALSE WITNESS THAT SPEAKETH LIES, AND HE THAT SOWETH DISCORD AMONG BRETHREN. KJV

Our emotions terrorize us. Whether we fantasize about them, act on them, or swat them down, they are always there, and always a danger to us. Our own emotions are a danger to us.

# God's Sexual Laws

I want to tell you, brethren, human sexuality is at the core of every sin of mankind. It came to my mind yesterday how you cannot remain in right standing with God if you go against his sexual laws. A nation cannot stand when it departs from God's sexual laws.

Sexual relationships between people have the power to make or break a person, a family, a nation, or the world. This is the reality nobody wants to hear. If you try to understand what I am about to say with your carnal mind, you will get it all wrong.

The reason human sexuality, the virtue of the woman, in particular, more than the man, either makes or breaks a person, a family, a nation, or a relationship, is because the woman has the ability to give birth to something which will continue to grow and expand, whether it is Godly or ungodly.

Brethren, please put your spiritual hat on, and tune up your spiritual ears. How we deal with human sexuality is very important, because it is not of God. God says we can have sex in marriage while we are down here in spiritual Babylon under wormwood judgment, but there is no marrying or giving in marriage in heaven.

### Matt 22:30 – *No Marriage In Heaven*

**30** FOR IN THE RESURRECTION THEY **NEITHER MARRY, NOR ARE GIVEN IN MARRIAGE,** BUT ARE AS THE ANGELS OF GOD IN HEAVEN. KJV

Human sexuality is not of God. The true sexuality is between God and man. You can engage in human sexuality without destroying yourself, and your children, your grandchildren, your great grandchildren, and the whole nation, if you keep it within God's standards. As soon as those laws fall apart, when they are no longer complied with, the end of it is nothing less than destruction for the individual, for the marriage, for the family, for the nation, and for the world.

This is because the body belongs to Satan, and the pleasure of the body is Satan's vehicle to destroy those who engage in sexual excess or forbidden sexual acts. God says you can use your body sexually within marriage according to his Law. A satisfying sex life without any negative consequences in the present or in future generations is a privilege and a gift from God. Where the privilege is abused, God's protection is lost and Satan will tyrannize you, or your descendants, unto destruction. Who is Satan? Satan is the internal spiritual force which drives the emotions of fallen mankind. *Freud* called it the *id*.

God is a Spirit, brethren. He is not your body. Your body is God's house.

### Jn 4:24 – *God Is Spirit*

**24** *GOD IS A SPIRIT*: AND THEY THAT WORSHIP HIM MUST WORSHIP HIM IN SPIRIT AND IN TRUTH. **KJV**

### 1 COR 3:16 – *TEMPLE OF GOD*

**16** KNOW YE NOT THAT **YE ARE THE TEMPLE OF GOD**, AND THAT THE SPIRIT OF GOD DWELLETH IN YOU? **KJV**

### 1 Cor 6:13 – *No Fornication*

**13** MEATS FOR THE BELLY, AND THE BELLY FOR MEATS: BUT GOD SHALL DESTROY BOTH IT AND THEM. NOW **THE BODY IS NOT FOR FORNICATION**, **BUT FOR THE LORD**; AND THE LORD FOR THE BODY. **KJV**

Sexual purity is absolutely essential for every kind of victory in life. Do not be deceived into believing people who are living outside of God's laws are prospering even if that appears to be the case. They may be fine now, but what about tomorrow?

# Selective Morality

I want to tell you what I heard Glenn Beck say the other day. He was counselling his radio audience, saying, *you have to get yourself straight with God. Hard times are coming, and the only thing that will save you is virtue within yourself. How you deal with other people, how you spend your money, whether you help the poor, whether you have mercy on the sick, on those that are in trouble, determines your degree of morality.* That is what he was telling everybody. *Love your neighbor, be prepared to help your neighbor. If you are not living right, you will not survive the judgment that is coming.*

I will take what Glenn said a step further. I am saying you can give to charity, build your neighbor's house, feed the poor and do everything Glenn is suggesting you do, but if you are in fornication, adultery or any kind of sexual sin, you will not survive the judgment. I have heard Glenn speak out about adultery, but I do not recall hearing him say anything about fornication or pornography. He clearly accepts homosexuality.

The foundational behavior which will make or break you when judgment falls upon the nation and the whole world is the purity of your sexual state. Jesus, the one who connects us to God, will not join himself to anyone who is actively engaged in sexual sin, and Scripture alone is the final arbiter which defines sexual sin.

### 1 Cor 6:9-10 – *No Homosexuality*

> [9] KNOW YE NOT THAT THE UNRIGHTEOUS SHALL NOT INHERIT THE KINGDOM OF GOD? BE NOT DECEIVED: NEITHER **FORNICATORS, NOR IDOLATERS, NOR ADULTERERS, NOR EFFEMINATE, NOR ABUSERS OF THEMSELVES WITH MANKIND,**

> [10] NOR THIEVES, NOR COVETOUS, NOR DRUNKARDS, NOR REVILERS, NOR EXTORTIONERS, SHALL INHERIT THE KINGDOM OF GOD. **KJV**

Brethren, it is not my intention to pick Glenn Beck apart. He is one of my political teachers. I thank God for him, but I disagree with him on the issue of what will get you through the hard times. All the altruism in the world will not negate sexual sin.

I heard Glenn talking about abortion the other day. He was commenting on a Congressman who described himself as personally pro-life, but did not believe he had the right to force his beliefs on other people. Glenn did not agree and his reasoning went something like this:

> I can see you saying that you do not believe in digging for gold in California, but if it is your personal preference I will not try to stop you. But I do not see how you can believe that abortion is murder, but you will not violate someone's right to commit murder. Does this country not punish murderers?

This is what I say to you: **Hard times are coming and individuals will be stripped to different degrees of everything they can hold onto.**

The Scripture says everything which can be shaken will be shaken. What does that mean? It means everything you rely on, your money, your doctor, the people who love you (human beings need affection), everything t you rely on to meet your needs in this world, will be shaken, and **shaken** means **taken away**. The only thing you will have to stand on which will give you hope of having your needs met in the crisis is your virtue before God. I think Glenn and I might agree on that. If we do, then the only issue on the table between us is the definition of **virtue**.

# Virtue

Brethren, the Scripture is clear, sexual purity is the root of God's virtue and righteousness. God does not join with you when you are in fornication. You can give away thousands of dollars, do every good work known to man, but he will not join with you when you are in fornication.

I can hear the crowd screaming, *that old fashioned woman, she is crazy!* I am not crazy. I know what God is telling me. Marriage does not protect you from the Scriptural prohibition against unclean sexual acts. There are sexual acts God says are unclean and practicing these acts, with partners of the opposite sex, or with partners of the same sex, whether you are married or unmarried, attracts ungodly powers to you which God will not join with.

The Lord Jesus Christ (who is joined to Jehovah) joins with your spirit to save your spirit, and he joins with your emotions to save your soul or your personality. He will not make that union… he will not begin to cleanse you until you are willing to give up the scripturally prohibited acts you are presently engaging in. He will not join with your sin.

# Supernatural Provision

If, God forbid, the world begins to experience the crisis many are predicting, and the only way to get food is through a supernatural union with the Lord Jesus Christ (who joins us to Jehovah), he will not join with the unclean spirit in you. He will not join with you to feed you supernaturally.

Does this mean a mean old God is picking on you because you are gay, or because you are in heterosexual fornication? No! Not at all! Every soul has a lock on it and there is only one key which fits the lock. There is a key and there is a lock. Jesus is the key that is the feeding tube, and he only fits into one particular soul lock. If you are in active sin, particularly sexual sin, the soul lock within you changes its form and Jesus, the key that feeds you God's food, will not unlock your locked soul.

God wants to save everybody. He wants to feed everybody. We must have the spiritual mechanism within us which receives his deliverance, his salvation, his food, his help, in whatever form it comes, in the days of crisis.

Two specific spiritual elements must join together to rescue us: The Lord Jesus is one and the other is a state of preparedness in the human being called *Christ Jesus*. The Lord is the male, the key to the lock, and the locked soul is the female.

There must be a door to the soul that receives the Lord Jesus, the key to Jehovah's provision, but Jesus, Jehovah's key, will not join with sexual impurity. I am telling you Jesus will not join himself to your sin, because the key he is will not fit in the keyhole of your locked soul.

The soul lock inside of us is the mechanism which feeds us supernaturally when the key enters in. It is the point of union between the Lord Jesus (who is attached to Jehovah) and Christ

Jesus within us which channels the food from a spiritual dimension inside of us.

The Scripture calls this provision *manna*. *The Zohar* tells us this spiritual substance, this *manna*, has the potential to become anything we may need because it comes from such a spiritually high place it can be considered *generic spiritual material*. Spiritual substance can become anything the mind is strong enough to form.

### Soncino Zohar

NOW THE MANNA WAS LIKE CORIANDER (gad) SEED.

Said R. Jose: 'The term gad (lit. troops) signifies that **the manna had the virtue of inducing propagation**. It implies further that in the same way as the seed of Gad took their portion in another land, [Tr. note: i.e. outside the border of the Holy Land proper, in Transjordania.] so the manna hovered over Israel outside the Holy Land.

We may also explain the words to mean that it was white in appearance, like coriander seed, and coagulated when it reached the atmosphere, and was transmuted into material substance[Tr. note: i.e. out of its ethereal state.] inside the body. [Tr. note: Al. "it was absorbed by the body", i.e. without leaving any waste, as with material food. v. T.B. Yoma, 75b.] AND THE APPEARANCE THEREOF AS THE APPEARANCE OF BDELLIUM, to wit, it was white in colour like bdellium, this being the colour of the Right in the supernal sphere.' (**Soncino Zohar**, Vol V, p 217 (Numbers 155b))

# Good Manners

You can call me old fashioned if you like, but I am not old fashioned. *You* are ignorant of God's ways and *you* are ignorant of the spiritual principles which produce prosperity and life. Jehovah wants to release the flood gates of prosperity and safety into every level of your locked soul through the Lord Jesus Christ, but you must understand what you must do to receive it.

I encourage all of you, one more time, to start learning good manners, if you do not already practice them. Say *please*, say *thank you*; hold the door for people. Gentlemen, relate properly to the ladies. Defer to those who are older than you and to whoever has authority over you. It does not have to be an old, old person. If you are 30 and they are 40, defer to them. Give them the seat. Recognize these differences among people and act accordingly.

This state of mind which produces good manners is essential if you hope to receive Jesus, the key which unlocks your soul. It is that very mind-set which creates a righteous spiritual structure, a spiritual keyhole which matches the righteous key of the Lord Jesus Christ and attracts him in your hour of need.

But, to the degree you think and behave otherwise, the spiritual keyhole, the soul opening which fits the key of the Lord Jesus Christ, will not be constructed within you and the Lord Jesus, the key which unlocks your soul to feed it, will be driven far away from you.

# Respect Is Restraint

Years ago, in the days of prudery, according to those who think I am out of touch, a young man would refuse to have sex with a woman he loved because he respected her. Does that attitude exist anywhere today? Young women should not have to resist pressure from their dates. They should not have to contend with someone they care about trying to break down their will like in the movie *Splendor in the grass*.

Young men, if you think pressuring a woman to engage in any degree of sexual activity, even kissing, when she is reluctant to do so is acceptable, you are mistaken. It is not acceptable to God for a man to pressure a woman until she yields. In your ignorance, you are committing a serious sin. It is ungodly to deliberately create a conflict in anyone.

You must strive to control the seven emotions of your fallen nature because in many instances they oppose your best interests. When the Lord Jesus Christ joins himself to your human spirit and Christ Jesus appears within you with power, the lusts of the flesh, the seven emotions of the fallen nature, will be rendered idle. They will be swallowed up by the Spirit of Christ and blended into the energy which produces eternal life, the spiritual blood supply of Christ Jesus, your higher soul, and they will no longer be able to tyrannize you.

# Bad Things Happen Sometimes

Jehovah created evil, but he never intended for the evil to do evil deeds.

### Is 45:7 – *God Is Sovereign*

> 7 I FORM THE LIGHT, AND CREATE DARKNESS: **I MAKE PEACE, AND CREATE EVIL**: I THE LORD DO ALL THESE THINGS. **KJV**

Evil, when it is joined to Jehovah's breath, in that compilation, in that unity, in that singularity, serves a positive function. The evil Jehovah created was intended to be balanced by his breath of life, and made useful to the creation.

Evil becomes powerful enough to tyrannize the weaker elements of creation only after it separates from Godly authority and cleaves to a destructive force. This is a spiritual principle which is true for every human being.

If we attach ourselves to God through the Lord Jesus and to righteous people, and if we set Godly goals for ourselves, we can have a very positive life. If we do not attach ourselves to God, and we choose the wrong friendships, the wrong people, bad things can happen. It is all about who you attach yourself to.

Sometimes men and women are attracted to members of the opposite sex, or members of the same sex, who are very bad for them. If we make the wrong choices and form the wrong attachments, bad things can happen. God forbid, one can wind up on drugs, as an alcoholic, or in jail. Brethren, bad things happen in this world.

# The Unlocked Soul

First you attach yourself to God through a relationship with the Lord Jesus Christ. Then you recognize any weaknesses, any attractions which you have to people who are bad for you. Once you recognize the bad choices you have made, the power of the Lord Jesus Christ will help you to begin to resist your attraction to ungodly people and you will begin to be attracted to spiritually healthy people.

Lust is more than sexual lust, but sex is the foundational drive of mankind. We must control our sex drive and our sexual choices and activities. They can and simply must be controlled or they will tyrannize you until they destroy you.

Listen to these promises from God, brethren:

### 2 Pet 1:3-4 – *Life & Godliness*

3 ACCORDING AS HIS DIVINE POWER HATH GIVEN UNTO US ALL THINGS THAT PERTAIN UNTO **LIFE AND GODLINESS, THROUGH THE KNOWLEDGE OF HIM** THAT HATH CALLED US TO GLORY AND VIRTUE:

4 WHEREBY ARE GIVEN UNTO US EXCEEDING GREAT AND PRECIOUS PROMISES: THAT BY THESE YE MIGHT BE PARTAKERS OF THE DIVINE NATURE, HAVING ESCAPED THE CORRUPTION THAT IS IN THE WORLD THROUGH LUST. **KJV**

*2 Pet 1:3 - AT: He has given us all things that pertain to life and godliness by his divine power, through the knowledge of [Jesus] who has called us to have his opinion and the highest standards of uprightness, beginning with our sexual standard and spreading out to every other aspect of our relationships. ATB*

*According as his divine power has given us all things that pertain to life and godliness, through a knowledge of him...* by studying Jesus, who he is and what he said, and by having his life in us, we receive the power of life and godliness.

We do not have to remain in a spiritually low place. *...through a knowledge of the one that has called us to have his opinion.* God is revealing his mind, which is his opinion, to the world through Jesus Christ. Jehovah wants us to have his mind, but we must first learn to distinguish between God's opinion and the opinion of the animal nature. We know we have acquired the mind of God when we are able to distinguish between the two natures and reject the animal nature.

# The Corruption of Virtue

*Virtue* means, *moral excellence, goodness and righteousness.*

If it is pointed out to you that your opinion is the opinion of the animal nature and you will not reject that opinion, you are denying yourself the opportunity for life and godliness through a knowledge of how Jesus escaped from the powers which rule this world. Jesus is Jehovah's righteous mind. You must turn against the internalized enemy within yourself, your carnal mind, and align your thoughts with the mind of Christ.

We must have virtue in business, virtue in human relationships, virtue between students and teachers, virtue between employers and employees, virtue between neighbors, virtue between relatives, virtue between ourselves and people who do not respect us… virtue. God is looking at who we are in the crisis.

*2 Pet 1:4 – AT: Whereby [these] exceeding great and precious promise are given unto us: that by [the Son of God who] escaped the corruption that is in the world through lust, that you [too], might be partakers of the divine nature ATB*

*Whereby are given unto us exceeding great and precious promises: that by these…*

The word *these* is talking about the sons of God. *…that by these…* people who manifest the *virtue* of God to you through the Lord Jesus Christ. These who are examples to you of righteous behavior amongst human beings ...*that by these you might be partakers...*that by following their example, *you might be partakers of the divine nature, having escaped the corruption that is in the world through lust.*

*2 Pet 1:3-4 – AT:*

**3a** *[Jehovah] has given us everything that pertains to life and godliness*

**4c** *[So that] you, [too], might be partakers of the divine nature*

**3b** *Through a knowledge of [how Jesus,*

THE ONE] WHO HAS INVITED US TO HAVE HIS OPINION AND THE HIGHEST STANDARDS OF UPRIGHTNESS,

BEGINNING WITH OUR SEXUAL STANDARD AND SPREADING OUT TO EVERY ASPECT OF OUR RELATIONSHIPS WITH OTHERS,

**4a** *Escaped the corruption that is in the world through lust, [which is*

**4b** *The very reason why these] exceeding great and precious promises are given to us.*

*ATB*

Corruption of our virtue starts with sexual lust, which is the driving force, but lust is everywhere. Lust for money, lust for self-esteem, lust for position, lust to dominate, lust to control, lust to possess, lust to punish. Every single one of those lusts has its expression in our sexuality in one way or another.

Human sexuality is very psychological and very emotional. It is not just a physical exercise, which is what is being taught in many of our schools and colleges today.

I heard a conversation between two college students recently. They were talking about getting together to have casual sex because they both needed it. They were not boyfriend and girlfriend or in love with each other. They were discussing their physical needs alone. I read recently about how this behavior is going on today, and it is more prevalent among women than among men. How sad!

# Table of References

# ABOUT THE AUTHOR

Sheila R. Vitale is the Spiritual Leader, Founding Teacher, and Pastor of Living Epistles Ministries (*LEM*) and Christ-Centered Kabbalah (*CCK*). A brief history of Pastor Vitale and the unique two-pronged ministry that the Lord Jesus Christ gave her charge over (*LEM/CCK*) is encapsulated below

She moves in the offices of Teacher of Apostolic Doctrine, Prophet, Evangelist and Pastor, has an international following, and has been expounding on the Scripture through a unique spiritual lens for nearly three decades. She has written more than 50 books based on the Old and New Testaments including *The Kabbalah of The 1ˢᵗ Epistle of John* and *the Crime of the Calf* (OT) and *The Three Israels* and *Jesus and The Learned Jew* (NT*).* She has also rendered original spiritual interpretations of Biblical texts such as *The Prophesies of Daniel According to Kabbalah, Chapter 11,* and *The Noah Chronicles.* Her unique, Multi-Part Message style is seen in *CCK* Serial Messages such as Reincarnation vs Transmigration (22 Parts) and Exodus, Chapter 32 (26 Parts). Each Part of a Multi-Part Message Series can also be enjoyed as a complete and independent study. In addition, she has defined, explained, illustrated and demonstrated hundreds of spiritual principles throughout more than 1,000 CCK lectures.

Her signature work, however, is the three volumes of *The Alternate Translation Bible (ATB)*: *The Alternate Translation Of The Old Testament, The Alternate Translation of the New Testament* and *The Alternate Translation of The Book of Revelation. The Alternate Translation Bible* is a work in progress (*The ATB Project*). Accordingly, additional spiritual interpretations of both whole and partial Chapters are added from time to time, as they are rendered. The most up-to-date versions of *The ATB Project* may be found online at the *LEM and CCK* websites: *LivingEpistles.org and Christ-CenteredKabbalah.org,* respectively. *The ATB* is a *spiritual interpretation* of the Scripture and is not intended to replace traditional translations.

She also analyzed the Greek text of *The Book of Revelation* and preached extensively on it in the early years of *The ATB Project.* During that time she produced 197 distinct *Message Parts*, under 29 specific *Message Titles*, all of which deal with *The Book of Revelation.*

Pastor Vitale is an illustrator of spiritual principles, a researcher, a translator and a reviewer of the Modern Social Trends of Family and Culture, as they are revealed through TV programs (*The Sopranos*), movies (*The Matrix* and *The Edge of Tomorrow*), and plays (*Wicked*). She also writes for the CCK *Blog.*

She travels domestically, as well as internationally, preaching and teaching Judeo-Christian Spiritual Philosophy, and has donated Audio Message Libraries of her Lectures to ministries in Asia, Africa, Europe and North America.

Pastor Vitale serves *CCK* in a range of spiritual, educational, and administrative functions from *The Selden Centre*, *LEM/CCK* headquarters in Selden, New York. She is also a philanthropic individual who supports the *Lighthouse Mission (Patchogue, NY) and HGM – Mission of Hope – Haiti, and other* charitable organizations. She also supports community services such as the *Terryville Fire Department.*

In her spare time, Pastor Vitale enjoys watching movies, attending plays and partaking of cuisines from different cultures. An avid traveler, she has visited several countries in Europe and Africa as well as many cities in the United States.

# BEGINNINGS, INSPIRATION AND CALLING

Pastor Vitale began her spiritual journey as a child when her Jewish mother enrolled her in the Hebrew school of an Orthodox synagogue. She experienced the Spirit of God for the first time there in such a profound way that she wept. But after that, when she was only eleven years old, she became very ill and was taken to Mount Sinai Hospital in New York City. She almost died there and has battled with life-threatening health issues ever since. Nevertheless, a deep longing for God continued to pursue her until several years later when she desperately wanted to attend Yeshiva (Jewish high school), but could not. Her secular parents approved of her choice but were not able to afford the tuition.

Much later, after years of searching, she once again experienced the Spirit that had brought her to tears in the synagogue of her youth, but this time it was at *Gospel Revivals Ministries*, a Pentecostal church where Deliverance Ministry was emphasized. She desired to understand the Bible since she was a child, but Scripture was difficult for her and she struggled with the text. Nevertheless, she read one Chapter of the Bible every day until, one day, *her spiritual eyes opened* and she saw an angel holding a little book.

After that, she attended as many as five teaching services each week for about seven years, the latter part of which she edited *Pastor Holzhauser's* books. But several more years had to pass before *the eyes of her understanding opened even further* and she began to receive *Revelation Knowledge of the Scripture*. She understood at that time that the angel she had seen was the angel of Revelation 10:8.

After about seven years of learning *Deliverance Ministry* and *The Doctrine of Sonship* (*Bill Britton*) from *Pastor*

*Holzhauser,* she studied the Bible independently under the influence and direction of the Holy Spirit.

In **1988** she began teaching Apostolic Doctrine.

In **1990** she spent three months in Stony Brook Hospital where she recovered from an incurable disease, defeating premature death, once again, and went on to resume teaching and managing *LEM.*

In **1992** she journeyed to Africa for the first time where she was called to the office of Evangelist.

In the **mid-1990s,** she began to Pastor in addition to being a Teacher of Apostolic Doctrine, a Prophet and an Evangelist, thus, satisfying all five offices of *The Ministry of the Lord Jesus Christ to His Church.*

# LIVING EPISTLES MINISTRIES

Pastor Vitale was happy fellowshipping at *Gospel Revivals Ministries* but, eventually, she desired a deeper and more spiritual understanding of the Word of God. One day, after crying out to Jesus about her need, she was amazed to hear Him ask her if she would teach. Her initial response was that she did not see how it would be possible since she was already working a full-time job, despite her poor health. But after the Lord asked her for a second and then a third time, she reluctantly agreed, believing that He would empower her to do the job. Shortly thereafter, in the latter part of 1987, she began to teach her own brand of Judeo-Christian Spiritual Philosophy.

The Lord Jesus Christ named the work *Living Epistles Ministries* in 1988.

The first *LEM* meetings were casual and spontaneous gatherings of friends and fellow deliverance workers in Pastor Vitale's home. After that, they were held in the business office of one of the brethren. Pastor Vitale delivered her first formal message entitled *The Truth About Witchcraft in January of 1988,* followed by *The Seduction of Eve* in April of the same year. After that, she prepared and taught weekly messages including *Signs of Apostleship* and *Lazarus & The Rich Man. The meetings eventually* increased to two and then three each week.

Sometime after that, she learned that the Lord Jesus Christ was revealing spiritual principles from the Hebrew text of the Old Testament through her teachings, and those spiritual principles helped her to begin to unlock the mysteries of the New Testament, as well. Today she understands that the Scripture is a spiritual document that must be spiritually discerned if it is to be understood correctly, and calls that spiritual understanding *The Doctrine of Christ.*

# CHRIST-CENTERED KABBALAH

## Another Beginning

After about ten years of teaching *the Doctrine of Christ,* in or about the year 2000, while she was evangelizing in Greenville, South Carolina, the Lord Jesus Christ introduced Pastor Vitale to *Lurian Kabbalah.* At that time, the Spirit of God directed her to read and study the teachings of *Rabbi Luria,* as written by his student, *Chayyim Vital,* in *The Tree of Life: The Palace of Adam Kadmon.* She did not understand the text at first, but continued on, nevertheless, until *the eyes of her understanding opened.*

Shortly thereafter, she began to teach *Lurian Kabbalah* and eventually applied the spiritual principles of that system to her studies in the Old Testament under the *Living Epistles Ministries* brand. Sometime in or about the year 2001, however, the Lord Jesus Christ named her, then current teachings, Christ-centered Kabbalah (*CCK*), thereby dividing *Living Epistles Ministries* into two branches, each with its own website and digital representations. Each ministry has its own label, but both also share the *LEM/CCK* moniker.

## About CCK

*Christ-Centered Kabbalah* is a new, vigorous approach to spiritual maturity, ascension and rectification (justification) based on Pastor Vitale's original research in *the Hebrew text of the Torah*, *the Greek text of the New Testament* and *the Zohar*, one of the foundational books of *Philosophical Kabbalah*.

*CCK, an* integration of the *Doctrine of Christ* and *Lurian Kabbalah*, two Bible-based philosophical systems, offers a fresh perspective concerning Israel's resurrection and Adam's restoration to a higher estate than the one he fell from.

She has studied the authentic Jewish Kabbalah of several Rabbinic scholars, including *Moses Nachmanides (Ramban)*, *Moses Cordovero (Ramak)* and *Isaac Luria (The Ari) and* has read many of the English translations of their writings, including *Ramban's The Gate of Reward*, *Ramak's Pardes Rimonim (Orchard of Pomegranates)*, and *the* teachings *of the Ari*, as written by his student, *Chayyim Vital: The Gate of Reincarnations* and *The Tree of Life: The Palace of Adam Kadmon*. Pastor Vitale attributes her ability to understand and teach authentic *Jewish Kabbalah* and *Christ-Centered Kabbalah,* which she believes is beyond the grasp of the human mind, to *The Lord Jesus Christ*.

Pastor Vitale cautions her students about the dangers of *Occult Qabalah* and warns everyone with ears to hear that all Kabbalah is not kosher (authentic). Pastor Vitale teaches *authentic Jewish Kabbalah, which glorifies God* and shuns the *occult Qabalah of personal power*, which, all too frequently, is used to control unsuspecting persons, acquire wealth by spiritual power, or punish one's enemies.

## Media

*CCK* publishes a wide range of material, including books, e-books, spiritual interpretations of the Scripture and transcripts of Pastor Vitale's *Christ-Centered Kaballah* Lectures. Many of her transcripts and the entire *Alternate Translation Bible* may be viewed without charge on the *CCK Website* (*Christ-CenteredKaballah.org*).

She also has an *Author's Website* where all of her books, as well as several photographs of herself and a short biography are displayed (Amazon.com/author/SheilaVitale). Paperback and digital versions of *CCK* books may be purchased through *Amazon, Google Books* and *Barnes & Noble. CCK* also provides free videos of her live streams through YouTube: *@Christ-CenteredKabbalah),* and other Internet Plat-forms.

# PASTOR VITALE TODAY

Today Pastor Vitale continues to dedicate her life to teaching the spiritual principles of the Bible and focuses daily on studying, writing and preaching powerful messages from *The Selden Centre,* LEM/CCK's headquarters at Selden, New York.

# ABOUT MARRIAGE

## A Spiritual View of
## Marriage, Divorce & Remarriage

Sheila R. Vitale

Living Epistles Ministries

# ADULTERY

## Real & Spiritual Applications

Sheila R. Vitale
Living Epistles Ministries

**Christ-Centered Kabbalah**
**Sheila R Vitale,**
**Pastor, Teacher & Founder**
~ The Compleat Kabbalah ~
PO Box 562, Port Jefferson Station, New York 11776, USA
Christ-CenteredKabbalah.org *or* Books@Christ-CenteredKabbalah.org